Poetically
Intertwined

Poetically Intertwined

DAVID WRIGHT
ASHLEY ROSE BROWN

DIPS
Publishing

Poetically Intertwined

Published by DIP'S Publishing
Cleveland, OH

www.thinkforyourself.life

ISBN: 978-1-946818-00-3
Printed in the United States of America

I dedicate this book to Ashley Rose Brown. I dedicate this book to you because you are a woman that I have learned so much from. The woman that I have evolved into appreciating life with. Through our many ups and downs, our friendship has outlasted lust, love and anything else under the sun that can be named. You have put your trust in me with action! Where most would have come up with excuses, you put all you had into me. With you by my side, I was able to build up a successful company. Raise three children and learn who I truly am on the inside of myself. You inspire me to grow because all you try to do is grow yourself. I have watched you change. You went in as a young lady and you have emerged from the cocoon as a full grown, confident woman. I have watched you firsthand use the power for your benefit. As you learn, you receive; you are truly a lovely woman. I am so thankful that you came into our lives. Truly a blessing you are, have been and I pray, will always be.

Thank you forever, Ashley Rose Brown.

Contents

Poetically Intertwined

A family for Rose

I sit and watch, the children play outside
as their parents observe in delight.
I sit and watch, the interaction of the provider playing and
teaching the children along the way.
I sit and watch, the nurturer as she coddles the child after a fall.
I sit and watch, the love that the parents have for each child,
with respect to each's personality trait.
I sit and watch, the grandmother as she smiles with delight
watching the second and third generations interact joyously.
I sit and watch, the grandfather teach from what has been taught
from generation to generation, along the way.
I sit and watch, as the mother and father interact with one
another giving a soft touch then gentle kiss.
I sit and watch, the children play a game of hide and seek as one
counts down aloud for the other to hide.
I sit and watch, the children swing back and forth as the mother
and father take turns pushing.
I sit and watch, one sibling encourage the other while swinging
from one side of the monkey bars to the other.
I sit and watch, as the parents and children laugh and giggle,
racing from one end of the yard to the other.
I sit and watch, the interactions of each family member with one
another, as they portray a loving example of family.
I sit and watch in elation, as I observe, the bond, strength,
happiness and courage of my own family.

Make me a woman

Make me not see anger first. I want to be reasonable and upright, in all of my thoughts and ways. Make me a women. Let me guide myself and others. Of course my family first, into a way that will serve to motivate them; not to steal their spirit. Make me a women, let every life impacted by my spirit leave forever better then they came. Let me be remembered, only as a mother and a person that cares. Make me a women. Let me rise to whatever occasion that I face, with grace dealing with situations comfortably. As I am in my thought so will the movements in my life reflect. Make me a women. So that I can make others into women after me! I want to mold and shape others, to mold and to shape others. Only sharing of my self, a human tithe. Giving more than my 10 percent required because I am endowed with amazing abilities. I give to show my gratitude because I am truly thankful. Make me greater, make me stronger; make me a woman!

Looking through the glass

I see all of my mistakes crying out to me. As we talk, I know that it shouldn't be in here; but my choices are such as they are. Just know that everything thing I did and do, is for you. Maybe a job was a better choice, but we live and we learn. I accept responsibility for every mistake that I've committed, I just pray that you can forgive me. I wouldn't blame you if the lack of my presence, turned you against me. I wouldn't blame you, if anything, just know that I love you. Just know that my best good enough, or not; is all I had and all that I could put forth. You were, are and will forever be my inspiration. Looking through the glass I know that now, looking through the glass, I know that my life was a small price to pay. But looking through this glass, I know that you need me. I know that the weight of the effect of my absence in your life, could never be a small price to pay. I truly let this logic escape me, it wasn't until right now that I realized my errors; Looking through the glass.

Without me

Without me holding me back, I would have been a success a long time ago. It seems, that I always get in my way. I have made poor choices but can always remember the right way presenting itself; only I heeded not. I went my own way, knowing it was wrong. Without me in the way, years ago, I would have triumphed. My first mind has always given me brilliant advice, I just didn't take it. I have conversed with myself after the fact many a time, to remember the correct choice that came and was apparent. Only, I didn't follow. I heard my inner voice saying no, to a questioned posed; I ignored it. I told the voice to: be quite. With out me in the way, I would have never failed. But I was in the way; so I did. Over and over again. Without me, without me, without me. I am great and I vow now, to get out of the way so I can prove it. I will realize my destiny, I will be what I was always meant to be. My reality of greatness and Heaven like bliss, will be easily obtained—without me in the way!

Don't be sad

Don't be sad. You harbor and house so much pain when you are. What hurts you,? You are not alone, so many more have experienced similar if not the same things, as you. That pain does cut deep, but physically; it's over. It only now lives and has life in your mind. Again and again, you rebirth your hurt and ill feelings of yesterday, keeping them fresh as when they occurred. Yesterday you were helpless; a child. But today you are strong. Only if you know however, that all strengths are in your thoughts. Don't let them continue to win, don't let them keep abusing you still. Before they hurt you physically but now through thought, you hurt yourself. You turn that knife of persecution in your back. You continuously judge yourself, when then you were helpless but now your strong. Strong enough to stop the pain; caused by anyone. So stop the pain being caused—by you. Don't be sad, be able. Be able to understand that simple truth that will set you free.

That we guide our fate through thought
tho we aren't often bright enough to see.
That the thought I hold and reflect upon most
is the thought that makes up me.
I cry I ask I pray for help
but this truth isn't given or gained by wealth.
When you are sad you're sad because my friend
you are thinking those thoughts yourself.

The magic lamp

I use you, and get all that I want—always. The magic lamp, my thoughts; you are with me doing as I request. You keep me safe or in danger, whichever I choose. I summon my blessings as well as my curses, with my thoughts; my magic lamp. I plan and vow now, to use you always for my benefit. For my help and not my hurt. My magic lamp, I will begin respecting you and using you for that which you were meant: MAKING MY LIFE PERFECT!

Another day

Another day, here; above ground. I am blessed to be chosen. Another day, Another chance to excel, another chance to do good, another chance to help somebody. You have picked me, yet again. I can completely claim your favor because I am here; and that is all the proof that I need. Another day, I greet you with open arms; whatever yesterday's events were—I care not. I claim and command the favor that grants me dominion, and I am here another day to wield and express my power! To express it for the betterment and advancement of the kingdom! If doubters are convinced of your power, by what they see. This was the agenda, through what they have seen and felt if they be changed; then they have another day to get right! Another day—each may be our last. But as long as I am here being granted breath. If I wake up and put my feet on the floor; then I will learn and Serve, ANOTHER DAY!

The world is a circus

The world is a circus. Center ring is our consciousness, our thoughts had daily on display; for all to see. The world, this world, our world this place we're in. Constructed to both delight and to mystify. To inspire life and to cause death. Our thought serving as ring master, we amaze on lookers with the miracles that we perform. Making words into flesh, right before your very eyes. Cursing some, while blessings others, in front of always; a packed house. The world is a circus, and we are the ones; the only ones. Responsible for the starring acts that will be show cased. Remember, that there are children present; keep your thoughts pleasant. We want them to walk away bright eyed, not in tears. The world is a circus, come one come all!

When you don't like change

When you don't like change, you are forced to deal with the
same situations; day in and day out. Over and over and over
again. Things stay the same, when you don't change.
You look for ways out of the mess you're in
but no ways presented do you take.
You don't ponder but posture to those that onlook
like you're fed up, and in need of new.
But when the lights turn off and everyone's gone,
you go back to doing the same things you do.
That got you where your life is now, with no change or deviation set.
If you stay doing the same things that you've always done,
never different results but the same ones will you get.
So the man that won't change, lives his life in a lane of boredom
and being scared to fail.
A life without change may seem safe enough,
But that life has too much in common with hell.

While hurting on the insides

While hurting on the insides I smile to keep from crying. Exhibiting all the strength in the world, while on the inside I feel utterly helpless. I cry out and ask for assistance. But am afraid to let others know how deep down the pain travels and how truly hurting on the insides, I really am. With so much pain, anger and anguish, held inside of me. I always feel on edge, I'm often found seeking relief through anger and outbursts. While hurting on the inside, I appear unpredictable and unable to love—to others; judging from the outside. I just want to be understood and accepted, appreciated and loved; no different than any one else. But because of my character flaws, I'm ridiculed and abandoned; pushed away and gossiped about. If given a choice, when being created, would I have not asked to be designed differently? But no choice was given in the matter, so here my soul and I stand joined, glued at the hip. Looking just fine, While hurting on the insides.

Raise one

Before you would judge me as a parent and my ways, raise one. It's funny that all the theories in the world are thrown out of the window; when your forced to. I have learned to admit, not being correct. There is no thing easy, when you raise one. No talk is needed, only undying effort. All that you preach, will get to put into action; when you raise one! You will get to see, that it can be—but isn't always as easy as you may think. There is a lot of faith required when you raise one. Actions taken, not always the best results obtained but as they were perfect in the moment, I stand by them; my decisions one and all. Raise one, there is no off time or vacations able to be taken. Tough love, hurting both sides but needed to exact results. What a challenge, what mental fortitude it takes, what an honor it is; to raise one.

Young black and enlightened

America's nightmare has been described as a black man that doesn't care. If this synopsis be true, then that must mean that I and others like myself; are Americas dream! We are her salvation because we are led by an open mind and not the shackles of how it's always been done. We are the innovative, we are the Young Black and Enlightened. We know, because we are meant to know! To be or not to be, for that is the question! Well, I AM! I AM Young, Black and Enlightened; it won't be so easy to fool me anymore. I understand, and am no longer concerned; with being you. I am concerned with the restructuring of the model and scale used as a mold of comparison. The model and scale, that keeps us less and you more. That mental garbage, embedded in us. That we all lean on to justify mistreatment and to make it OK. I am Young, Black and Enlightened; make room, because change is coming!

They depend on me

They depend on me, how can I let them down? I buckle sometimes under pressure; to be put better. I bend but don't break, I may lean but I don't fold. How can I not be there, they depend on me. I must have and possess all the strength necessary to never let them down. But as they depend on me, I find myself depending on this feeling of strength; provided by them. So who truly, is depending on who? Yes, I do for them but it is the feeling provided by them, that heightens my abilities; enabling progress and success. So, as I do for them, they do for me! A natural circle of service and reciprocation. They depend on me and I them. What an honor it is to play my part, a father!

Fake it until you make it

Believe in things that are not, as though they were. Living in the end is the only true form of prayer, that will bring desired results. Talking on your knees is acknowledgement, not prayer. Believe in things that are not, as tho they were. You are allowed, for it is your birthright, what do you desire? Hint: that which you desire is the thing which you contemplate. The thing that which you ponder, with waking thoughts. You lament, torment and beat yourself. Or you exalt, expect favor and praise your existence. Fake it until you make it, living in the end is the only true form of prayer, that will bring desired results. When you imagine, better yet mentally conceive, you physically achieve. A man can only rise as high as his highest thought. Your highest thought has you currently where you are. What's your highest thought? Now multiply it by 10. Fake it, until you make it.

His story

His story is all I heard as a child. Hearing his story and constantly getting it engrained in my head, had me wanting to be him. Now, I understand that my story is where my importance in this universe lies for me. My story is packed with power, an ageless power. I am unstoppable, for centuries my car has been in park however. I will get moving, I just have to learn my story. In his story, I am made to look like a fool; instead of the master mason I am. For my ancestors designed the cosmos; masters at galactic masonry all. What is more regal than that? My story, wiped from the books; outlawed to all that knew the truth. Now, the truth at best is a fabrication. No longer even called truth, now they call truth—HIS STORY.

The present

The present, is a present to us all. Such a gift abundantly wasted, by everyone; so no blame is being placed. Only the thought of a different approach, a way to take advantage of the present. The present, the here and now. Endowed and bestowed upon each. Each second, able to be better than the last. If utilized correctly, our present can be such a gift. Effectively helping and bringing aid to others. Granting them with the present of providing. Rather to give a fishing pole than a fish. Greater it is to be not needed, than it is to be looked up to. The present, our daily way of making tomorrow better. Yesterday dictates our today's and tomorrow will be affected by—the present.

A letter to my son

I know that you feel like your right, and justified in your ways. I know you feel like your just following in my footsteps. As I was wrong like you, I see your error and know the pain that you are causing to YOURSELF! No one can suffer with you. We can watch, but that is all because true suffering is done on the inside. I can't help you there anymore because I'm not invited in. Your a man now, so I'm fine where I sit; on the outside of your life. I'm just aware of the road you travel. Only because I traveled it, only because I know how it ends. This is to my flesh and blood son. But as we all are one, every son under the sound of my voice is mine! So this is, a letter to my SONS!

Comfortable silence

Comfortable silence can't be shared with everyone. I can look into your eyes and not say a word. Communicating by my smile. Sitting, talking with you, sometimes I find myself just holding the phone. Comfortable silence can't be shared with everyone. But I share it with you; I can just be—with you. Never having to perform, or be on. Our connection is mutually shared. Often completing each other's sentences. I hope this bond is never broken! I know how much that you are worth to me. My dear, you are special because comfortable silence can't be shared with everyone.

I believe

I believe, and I always have. But before, I believed with my mothers eyes and heart. Now, I see the truth with my own. Now, I know, so now I believe. I believed before, but it's just different now. Now, I know what I believe in, and I know why I should. I believe because I am apart, I believe because you have given me a mind in which to do so. I believe because I would be lost; without my belief!

Homeless

Homeless, out here with no where to go. I have not been home in so long, I don't know where it is anymore. I'm looking up and down the streets where I think it is, but it's not there anymore. I don't even recognize any of the faces around here. Homeless, without a family or place to go. I hear a voice calling, I turn around and see, no one. Wait, that's my inner voice calling to me. As I answer, I hear it whispering, "This way." This way to where I ask? This way to home, to you! I followed my voice and found my home/myself inside of me. And now, I'm homeless no more!

Touching

We have finally arrived here, at this point; touching. I have wanted to put my hands on you many a time, but always exercised my control and showed restraint. Always wanting to be appropriate, I feel like I have been suppressing nature. Not any more, now we are touching. You feel just right, like a cloud. Your skin reminds me of what heaven must be like. I am so glad I waited for you to be ready. Rushing you, I may not have experienced this. You, allowing me to be next to you, means so much. At this moment in my life, there is no other woman I'd rather be touching. And I can honestly say, I hope this feeling lasts forever.

Risking my life

Have I been for all these years? Money, I believe you have gotten the better of me. If not for my education, what would I have. Since knowledge is power, I guess it wasn't a total wash. I have made myself better in thought but those late nights. The ones when I gave my all to gain you, grave yard chances taken; are an understatement. Because at points, my very soul seemed in jeopardy. I am done risking my life, it wasnt worth it. Indeed chances make champions but the numbers don't add up. For every one of me, there are 20 that lost. Who knows, if my success precipitated their choice. Risking my life, not any more; not for this. If you followed me before, follow me now! Together, we will find another way.

Neither do I

You don't feel the same way anymore? Neither do I. Truly you are no prize. As you complain, I find solace and escape in my mind. I have been ready to leave you, it is only for the children's sake I have remained this long. You heap onto me burden after burden, weight after weight. I have never buckled under the pressure because I am a man. I'm just tired of you, of this. You say that you hate me, your fed up and you no longer want this to work? Well my dear, Neither Do I!

My Sweet Life

Full of ups and downs, sometimes more downs than ups. For years I lived in My Sweet Life the valleys of this existence, we call life. A few times hovering, then taking flight, only to be brought crashing back down to reality. Thoughts like *Am I worthy?* Answers always in response like *I Am!* As things inevitably picked up and progressed in the direction opposite of negative, I had to think. I was prompted to ponder back upon those misfortunes and instances I lost, failed and struggled. I was forced to remember, in these times of abundance and plenty; what it used to be like. So I sat back and reminisced. About the times when I was so broke, if using the restroom cost a nickel; I would have had to throw up. Now I worry, care, complain, fret and fear not. My sweet life, designed for a King. Masterfully engineered, as if all the things that led me to this point were divinely orchestrated and part of the process. I'm thankful for my ups, my down's and my in betweens. My sweet life, expected and amazing all at the same time. My sweet life, lived to the fullest and appreciated everyday.

Justice /just us

We are here, all alone, just us. Seeking ...

What do we seek, amazing it is that fair treatment must still be asked for in this day and age. Children are children, misguided and headstrong. Yours, the same as ours. While news cameras and prisons follow our children, rehabs and second chances follow yours. It's hard to ask for freedom. Or even understand what it is, when you know; it's just us. Police MURDERING WHAT WE HAVE CREATED, hiding history even better than was done before. You say I place blame; true. Because YOU WONT STOP IT! You act as if it doesn't happen, like you deserve the perks in society you get. Yes you are to blame, for every perk, we lose a life. We live in a concentration camp amongst you. Stereotyping even our own, brain washed. Scared and in fear of what I see in the mirror. It's just us, just us against the world! For when you see me, you see ignorance. The washing of your brain, complete as well. Justice may have a different meaning for you. When I heard you talk about justice, I thought you were saying 'JUST US' REALLY QUICKLY!

Like I do

Do you really feel like I do? Do you love me, or do you just want to be friends. If so, I have to say goodbye. I can't take the waiting anymore. I have given up everything I have, gladly. I have no regrets! I just now know how hard I can love and how loyal I can be. Not to you because you were never mine. But I am loyal, to the thought of love. I let people pass me by, for my love of you. Not For You, because you don't feel like I do. But I did it for the thought, for the thought of being there, when it was time. I have learned so much about myself going through this. I thank you for not feeling...like I do. This friction has me to a fine point. I have gained wisdom through trial and tribulation. Thank you for helping me feel...LIKE I DO!

Addiction so rare

Optimistically thinking from day to day,
The addiction for my sacrifice will pave its way.
The way to my authentic goal,
For which I shall surrender my soul.
My addiction, is not that of an antagonistic nature,
But of a vivid portrait that one's eye clearly must capture.
Never to let anyone doubt my hard work and determination,
The chronic perseverance shall meet it's greater salvation.
I must say, I do feel weary and tired.
But, only success comes from being focused and inspired.
Yes, the struggle is very real,
But, only the strong have the dedication and will.
Yet, who is complaining?
The ups and downs and ins and outs, will only heed way to the
tenacious minds remaining.
If I'm taken through a journey of rejections to get that one, yes!
Then, I must fight through that journey to have many to
impress.
With faith endlessly watching over me,
The power of His word will guide and never forsake thee.
My addiction is oh, so rare,
That only a true addict, would find it positively fair.

Bully

If you stop talking about me, I promise to do your homework for
the rest of the year.
If you stop making me cry, I will give you my lunch money for
the next four years.
If you're, just nice to me, I will promise to always be your patsy.
I'm big, but why must you throw food and spit on me.
I don't have new clothes, doesn't mean that you throw change at my feet.
Just because my hair doesn't look as good as yours, please tell me
why you cut my hair off.
My skin isn't the same color as yours, so why must you call me names.
I am not cool like you, so why must you taunt me for being a geek.
You look at me in disgust;
You laugh at me as if I'm a clown;
I am not like you, so why can't I just be me.
Then again we do share a commonality;

I am a child, who didn't ask to be brought into this world just
like you;
I am an innocent child, living in this world, just like you. I have
endured too much pain and suffering from you, do you feel like
you ever get tired?
Well, I hope that you are because you will not see me tomorrow.
Because, for tomorrow is a new day,
tomorrow is my new day of hope.

From this day forward;
I will not let you talk about me,
I will not shed another tear,
I will not let you hurt me,
I will not let you spit on me,
I will not let you call me names, and
I will not let you laugh at me,
For tomorrow, brings my new hope and for tomorrow, you will
see me, for who I am, and not who you want me to be.

Delicate Rose

Exploding with compassion, fear, and joy,
For her beauty to only employ.
Happiness elates her smiling bloom,
But sometimes she's captured in an enclosed room.
The liberated petals on her stem, are descending from her core root,
The vibrant color that gives way, shall only be imprinted with
certain absolute.
Her roots, being the entire foundation of her development,
Always remembering, what led to her characteristic relevance.
Her thorns, so, are few,
But able to cause pain upon cue.
The natural aroma brings endless bliss,
So seductive that one will only miss...
Her stem is the pillar of an earthly green,
More beautiful than anything you'd ever seen.

Do not accept defeat

Do not accept defeat!
The ability to conquer, is the most powerful thing that one has.
Conquer your mind and you can obtain the world's most
wonderful treasures!
To conquer, is to gain control, through understanding the world
within yourself, The mindset to obtain even what may seem to
be the hardest, is actually the easiest. Look at yourself, what do
you see, I see God's most beautiful being,
God's being in every one of us, but is that what you see? Do not
let the external, what we have, take over your thoughts,
Think, say, suggest that is, commit, but only commit to the
happiness in your mind,
Only commit to the truth that, I think therefore, I will be his
image;
As opposed to subjecting yourself to the torments of negativity,
The negativity that consumes your thoughts, while helping you,
to accept defeat.

Fear within

Fear is the epitome of failure.
Fear binds to the thought of, I can't, I don't know how, it's too
hard or, it's impossible!
Fear will keep you from reaching what is meant to be.
As long as fear is fueled, it will overtake your conscious mind,
As long as you give hope to fear, it will begin to believe in you,
As long as fear can bind to you, like a leach, it will suck you dry.
Fear will manifest into stress, which in turn, will lead to
depression, sadness and negativity.
Instead of fear of the unexpected, take hold of the expected!
Expect each outcome to be in your favor,
Expect each outcome to be without doubt,
Expect the spoken word within, to be that of faith.
Fear not, of what could have, should have, or would have been,
but grasp the feeling of what will be now!

Fly

Fly away, little birdy!
The air is so sweet and pure,
It's getting cold outside.
Spring is gone, Summer has left, Fall is leaving and
Winter is coming.
The leaves on the trees are no longer falling and have departed.
The trees stand tall and bare, as if to be missing their essence.
But, do not despair,
There is still time before the trees are covered with snow.
Do not worry,
For spring will be present yet again!
Spread your wings and follow the North Star to a peaceful place!
Soar, gracefully, as your wings freely move to and fro.
The sky is clear, without any suppressing weather.
Yet again, I say, fly away little birdy, to that peaceful somber.

Free

I'm flying in the air, on a natural base.
As the wind, blows softly on my face
I'm slowly soaring through the sky,
Never to ask the question why.
I shall leave without another care,
As the blueness of the sky surrounds me so fair.
Gliding towards heaven's nest, with peacock colored wings,
The voices of the angels begin to sing!
Now free from human nature's sin,
Finally, letting go of my demons within.
The beauty, of freedom,
Has now, bloomed, yet another season.

Happiness elates

As the sun's ray's glow, in the sky,
I see your face from a mile high!
Your aroma fills the room with the most astonishing scent!
As to be expected with your grandeur, to accent.
Your stroll puts me at ease as to never rush,
Just the mere thought of your existence
brings my cheeks to a blush.
When you lay your hands on my face,
Your touch, takes my heart's beat, to an immediate race.
With your presence as my comfort zone,
I am never afraid to be alone.
With your mentality on a positive path,
My mind, is sure to pave way through the negative wrath.
Your words flow through the air like Bach's first composition,
Capturing me, with irrefutable intuition.
My future, seemed to be set with such uncertainty,
Before you arrived, into my life, to perfect my destiny.

Her love

My love for you, is like a mother's love at first sight,
I am your backbone, your foundation, your pillar,
No matter how congested the road has been,
I have remained in your lane until the traffic has cleared,
I am your woman and no one can take that away.
Despite the many enticing offers, I have always rejected.
The mere thought of you being mine has just been persuasion.
For you, I am bound by my loyalty,
I am bound by the devotion and faithfulness that I have spoken
into existence,
Tell me what you want and I'll get it,
Tell me what you need and you'll have it,
I was completely broken, but you gracefully and patiently pieced
me back together,
You have done so much for me, now it is time for me to do the same,
Yes, sometimes we disagree on things but in Love that is Life,
And in life that is love,
This is, my love's, safe haven, for your loves embrace!

Her tender heart

Crying out for someone to love me,
I gave my soul, but it did not suffice.
You could never hear my tender pain.
All of the talking, screaming, and loving, but you only heard
your heart so vain.
My heart was fascinated and gullible for yours,
My soul was an open plain
with nothing yet cultivated in a land so dry;
So dry, to leave one desiccated.
I acted as if everything was fine,
But it was only a façade, a façade for you, but why?
I have done everything that you asked of me plus one.
Even when, I thought that I was right you always reminded me
that I was wrong,
Even when, I did it the exact way that you did previously, I was
still wrong.
You made me think that I wasn't good enough for you,
You killed my pride with your hateful ways.
But soon, I learned that it was you who wasn't good enough for me.
I had become a lover to myself and
in conjunction a phenomenal woman!
Then again, I already was, I just had to be one with my inner self.
I was perfectly flawed without guidance;
And now, that I have seeked guidance, no barrier shall obstruct
my path again.

If I am you

If I am you, I cannot be me;
If I am you, this could never be.
If I am you, we would be alike;
If I am you, what would that be like.
If I am you, I would be predictable;
If I am you, how could that be acceptable.
If I am you, how could we possibly attract;
If I am you, how would we remain intact.
If I am you, would that be any fun;
If I am you, we could never be one.
If I am you, then you would have total control;
If I am you, I would never be whole.
If I am you, there goes my originality;
If I am you, then i will have no totality.
Huh, good thing that I am not you,
Because I love being me!

Innocence

Please, please, stop, I'm begging you!
I don't want to anymore! I can't, I'm just a child!
I am a child, who has been through so much pain from the
person who was supposed to love me,
But you don't love me because you don't see my tears,
You don't see the tears that pour down my face,
The tears that pour down my face every, night, when you come
into my room,
You don't hear the pain,
You don't feel the pain that I feel every night,
Every night, you take my innocence.
I hear the creaking of the floor outside of my bedroom,
While your shadow peeks from underneath my locked door,
How do you get in, I don't know,
Every night, to take my innocence,
My mother is in a deep sleep,
But you call it a drug induced coma, because she can't hear her
little girl's cries for help,
I try to tell her in the morning, but I'm just a child and I don't
understand a father's love you say,
Why don't you believe me mommy,
Why don't you believe your little girl,
Every night, he takes my innocence,
I bleed and hurt,

You say that it's a part of becoming a woman,
But I'm only 8,
How can I become a woman so young,
I told you about the first time that he tried to put his tongue in
my mouth,
But, you told me that it was an accident,
How so mommy, how can you accidently
put your tongue in a child's mouth,
That night you told him what I said
and that night was the first night,
Now, every night, he takes my innocence,
Mommy, you said that it was me and you against the world,
You said, that you would love me to the moon and back,
You said, that I was your baby forever,
You said, that I'll love you forever,
But how, when you don't believe me when I say,
"Your husband has been
Taking my innocence every night!"

It's me

Help me to understand,
To understand why you continue to let me feel this pain,
Feel the pain of your consistent evil ways,
Your evil ways that continue to walk all over me,
To walk all over me like the soles of your shoes,
Like the shoes on a poor man's feet without any rest,
Without any rest from the constant anger,
The constant anger that pushes me to run,
To run far away into the abyss,
Into the abyss of Satan's dark tunnel,
Satan's dark tunnel in need of a little light,
A little light if only just a glimpse,
If only just a glimpse for faith at the end,
For faith at the end of this dark tunnel,
Of this dark tunnel that seems to never end,
That seems to never end, but wait!
But wait, it's me, it's me, holding myself back from the light at
the end of the tunnel
From the light at the end of the tunnel to a new righteous me;
A new righteous me who is a whole me!
A whole, better, happier me
A happier me filled with forgiveness, dignity and loving myself,
Forgiveness, dignity and loving myself, forevermore!

It's ok

It's ok, that you don't love me anymore;
Yes, it is ok, that we don't share that adoration anymore.
Some things just get old with time and personalities change;
Habit has held us hostage for long enough.
I now understand, that it is ok to part;
I now know, that it is ok to say goodbye;
I now see, that it is ok to let go;
I now, comprehend the concept, of moving on.

My child

You are my light, my joy and my everything.
Just look how disciplined you have become,
Remembering everything that was taught throughout your years,
Has helped you to understand this world.
Never walking down another's path,
always maintaining your own lane,
It is your determination that encourages others not just your peers,
But everyone, that you have encountered through your lifetime.
You are my everything and through you I have accomplished one
of life's most astonishing goals,
To raise my child who has respect, wisdom, and integrity.
You are my unparalleled strength, "To infinity and beyond," is
what we used to say.
Whenever I felt like life was unbearable I looked at you,
I looked at you and reminded myself what life was all about,
A mother's love is unconditional,
no matter how hard it may be to raise you,
No matter how difficult the journey may be,
I unfailingly, managed through all of the tears and struggles,
Knowing that there was always a radiant glow
at the end of our journey,
My love will always be, unlimited, unrestricted, unreserved and
unquestioning, for you, my darling dear.

My thoughts

The world is an open circle,
but every time you turn around it's a closed square.
Where has everyone gone, does it feel as if you are lost
and can't find your way through the rubbish.
There is so much confusion, so much anger,
so much aggravation tripled with disappointment.
Will there ever be an opening in this box, if only to be an acute hole.
The acute hole to a peace of serenity within this troubled world.
Do the innocent always wreak the havoc of the evil's mentality?
Shall the innocent always get punished for a being's vice?
Even the prayer warriors don't possess the materials
to be, oh so positive.
As the devil is constantly preying on the weak.
I beg of you, please be strong enough to flout that attraction.
Take your mind to that field of dreams that will not allow any
damaging thoughts.
Take your mind to a presence of glee!
Allow your pool of untroubled thoughts
to drown out your troubled ones...
Allow your pool of untroubled thoughts
to destroy a troubled one before entering.
Open your mind to the influence of control.
Open your mind to the power of thought's unequivocal, mastery!

Just stop for a moment

Just stop for a moment,
Look, listen, feel, smell.
Open up your mind, body and soul, to what nature brings!
The beauty and calmness of the world stands bold, for our eyes
to be enchanted!
Take in the natural aroma of the evergreens,
Observe the endless allure of the sky's hue,
Listen, to the birds sing, as they soar high above the trees,
Feel the gentle breeze, upon your face, like a mother's touch of
love's embrace.
Take heed, to what has been put forth for a sense of tranquility.
Welcome the rain droplets that feed the earth,
Recognize the rain, as part of nature's most plentiful gifts.
Unlock your heart to the peace and serenity of Mother's Nature.
Capture the sun's rise and fall as the start and
end of a gracious day!

One

You are me, I am you, we are one.
We are a quarter, we are a half, we are three quarters,
pieced into a whole.
I am your support, you are my pillar.
Whatever I am so are you.
Whatever you are so am I.
We are bound by faith, we are bound by God.
We have evolved as a pair, we are enveloped in each other's body,
mind and soul.
We have attached physically, mentally and emotionally.
If you do, so do I, if I do, so do you.
Your flaws plus my flaws do not make us perfect,
Your perfections plus my perfections does not make us flawless,
but it does form a bond, that is perfectly made of flaws, as one.
To have and to hold, forever, our vows to each other.
To hold and to have, always, we have vowed to be one.
Even death will not part us, for it is only the mere presence
that no longer exists.
A husband to his wife and a wife to her husband.
We, as one, listen to each other's words and gestures
I know you for who you are, and you know me for who I am.
A mere distraction shall not separate our hold,
Our communication is as one,
No fault shall be blamed,
And no battle shall be fought alone,
For as a whole, we live, together, in unison as ONE!

Our gift

We as women shall not put ourselves out,
For we are God's gift without a doubt.
Beauty comes from deeply within,
Why should we surrender our body's to win.
The peril and sacrifices that our sister's endured,
Scarcely gave way for our freedom procured.
We were given our special quality
that gives us equality within society,
Which in turn helped give way to a complete sense of prosperity.
We will value ourselves as a whole,
And stand tall in order to reach our absolute control.
We were created to possess a genuine nurture,
To continue to form our societal sculpture.

Respect

All I ask for is a little respect.
Can you even hear that, or just neglect?
The selfishness of your beating heart,
Will turn around to stab you like a dart.
Your lies are an ongoing stream,
That seem to be so hard to wean.
The habitual tricks that you play,
Never have really, seemed to give way.
The sky was an infinite way of my love toward you,
But you never processed the heart so true.
All I ask for is a little respect.
Will you ever be able grasp that concept?

Security blanket

We all, possess a distinctive but similar quality
that is not that hard to grasp,
To love what is internally present for all,
Yet, we still look at what is external, for security.
We all, have that one thing that is used every night,
a security blanket, to comfort our damaged minds.
Whether love, money, or possessions,
they all seem to fill that black hole within.
Yet, if we take our blanket away, we feel unhinged, from the world,
We fold into ourselves; we become completely engulfed into
sadness, due to our external perception of security,
We feel, as if the external will make us whole,
We perceive, the external as a reflection of our happiness,
We feel, that the external will turn the imperfect into the perfect,
We perceive, that love, for the external,
will help us love the internal self,
We feel, that it will make us a stronger more powerful being,
When in all actuality, the true power, begins deep within oneself.
It begins with the completed understanding of loving yourself
with all certainty!

Tears

Tears, are flowing down my face,
Only to burn the skin that lay in place.
Oh how they hurt so bad,
Will there ever be a time when I'm not feeling so sad.
Yet so many forms of tears,
Why have the ones that I've dropped,
followed me throughout these years.
If only to stop the silent cries from falling,
Will my body and mind ever be in harmony to hear my calling?
Can you keep me away from such painful drops?
Or will there continue to be so many sorrowful knots.

The love that I want

I want that not so convenient love,
That love, that wakes me up in the middle of the night love.
I want that we don't give a damn love,
That love, that doesn't care,
if we are seen kissing or touching in public love.
I want that constant affection love,
That love, that never fades even on the rainiest of days love.
I want that best friend love,
That love, that makes me the first person that you go to whether
happy or sad love.
I want that respectful love,
That love, that puts me first and never raises his voice or hand to
chastise me love
I want that inseparable love,
That love that is strong like a knot love.
I want that no secrets love,
That love, that is always truthful and not hiding lies love.
I want that non resentful love,
That love, that corrects and forgives a mistake love.
I want that encouraging love,
That love, that will give support, hope and confidence love.
I want that committed love,
That to sustain and embrace,
Whether we're rich or poor,
Whether we're ill or well,

To love, to treasure,
Until death shall part us,
That fidelity love,
That family love,
That:
L-Loyal
O-Optimistic
V-Valued
E-Everlasting
LOVE!

To know, to love, to understand

I do not know you as I thought that I once did,
But to truly know someone is to love them,
And to truly love someone is to know them.
Have you ever really loved someone
to know them or known someone to love them?
To know someone is to be aware of through observation;
To have developed a bond with through interaction and time, but
To love someone is to have an immense feeling
of unfathomable affection;
To have a deep romantic or sexual attachment to.
When you think about yourself do you think about them?
Do you think about them with a smile held strong?
When you merely speak their name
does it bring butterflies to your stomach?
Does it bring a sense of security to an unfavorable day?
When you see their face are you held speechless by their beauty,
Are you held speechless by the beauty of that person within?
It's knowing that true being that leads you to love them or is it?
Then again, how can I know you to love you or love you to
know you, if I never really understood the person deep within?
To understand you, is to know and to love where you have come
from, where you are now, and where you are going.